# Never Settle For Par

Wade R. Conway

Copyright © 2018 Wade R. Conway

All rights reserved.

ISBN:1985128209
ISBN-13:9781985128200

# DEDICATION

This book is dedicated to my devoted, beautiful and hard working wife, Stephanie, who had to suffer through all of the late nights with me working, and me working while on vacation and with me taking calls while we were at dinner or at another family activity. Without your love, patience, and understanding this book would have never happened. I love you bunchies!

I also want to thank my Mom and Dad, Barbara and Jerry, who supported me through all of the tough decisions that they allowed me to make. They gave me the strength, confidence, and the latitude that allowed me to make mistakes and learn from them and to forge my own way and to stand on my own with confidence knowing that they had my back. I can't thank you enough for that. I love you so much.

# CONTENTS

|   | Acknowledgments | i |
|---|---|---|
| 1 | Visualization | 1 |
| 2 | Keep in the Present | Pg #9 |
| 3 | Be Yourself | Pg #11 |
| 4 | Outwork Your Competition | Pg #13 |
| 5 | The Pre-Swing Routine ~Scripting | Pg #17 |
| 6 | The Fundamentals GASP | Pg #18 |
|   | a. Grip ~ Verbiage | Pg #18 |
|   | b. Aim ~ Goal Setting | Pg #19 |
|   | c. Stance/Posture | Pg #22 |
| 7 | Alignment ~ Your Why | Pg #23 |
| 8 | The Waggle ~ Setting the Tone | Pg #27 |
| 9 | Caddies and Coaches | Pg #32 |
| 10 | Life on Tour ~ The Home Team | Pg #35 |
| 11 | Focus in Focus Out | Pg #37 |
| 12 | Find Your Niche | Pg #39 |
| 13 | Practice with Purpose | Pg #42 |
| 14 | Giving up Control ~ The Assistant | Pg #45 |
| 15 | Play It Where It Lies ~ Integrity | Pg #50 |
| 16 | Confidence | Pg #52 |
| 17 | Don't Beat Yourself | Pg #56 |
| 18 | The 19th Hole ~ Conclusion | Pg #57 |

Wade R. Conway

# ACKNOWLEDGMENTS

Thank you, thank you, thank you to Tim Davis for believing in me and holding my feet to the fire. I have had a goal to write a book for years and was planning on doing it by the end of the year, but you pushed me to do it by the end of the month and gave me the time to do it and the idea for what to base it on. Thank you for your friendship, mentorship, trust, and leadership. You rock!

Thanks goes to Peter Pessetto for the book title and to all the other Coaches at Movement Mortgage for your ideas, inspiration, and support.

Ken Maynard, my friend and brother, thanks for the awesome cover, your advice, revisions, and editing, and for your friendship and encouragement over the last 20+ years. I love you brother.

Thanks to our Lord and Savior Jesus Christ, through whom all things are possible.

# 1 VISUALIZATION

It was a windy day in West Texas, which was nothing new, but it was unusually windy even for West Texas. They say the average wind speed in Amarillo, Texas, is around eighteen miles per hour. I think that is because in some seasons it doesn't blow much at all and the others it blows more like forty miles per hour.

On this particularly windy day, a young man was faced with a very challenging situation. He was on one of the last holes of a big golf tournament. It was a tricky par four and the wind was blowing a gale force straight into his face. Wind coming from that direction and that magnitude could double or triple any side spin on a golf shot and on this certain hole there was a barbed wire fence serving the dual purpose of separating a cow pasture from the golf course and as out of bounds on the right side of the course. On the left side was a street and just beyond the street was a subdivision, also out of bounds. The situation was that it was the second to last hole of the tournament and the young golfer needed to play level par or better for the last few holes to win the match and qualify for the next level. He had played this hole a few times before and it had been a disaster. He had once stood on the tee in the middle of one of the best rounds that he'd had in his youth as a freshmen golfer playing on the varsity team. He proceeded to hit his tee ball out of bounds on the left. He teed up another and hit it out on the left again. He repeated this twice on the right side as well. Each time before he hit, he still had the image of the ball going out on the last shot. Hitting 8 off the tee, he holed out in five shots netting a thirteen and ruining his round and the chance to advance to the regional tournament. But this time, THIS TIME it was going to be different. He was armed with the knowledge that his brain was preprogrammed not to give him what he wanted, but what he could VISUALIZE.

Visualization can tame the toughest tee shot into the wind, the fiercest 200-yard approach shot over water to a rock hard slick green protected on all sides by deep high-faced bunkers. It can drop ten-foot putts to win a five spot from your buddies or a five-foot putt to win the Masters. It can make the seemingly impossible possible simply by being able to see it. One of the most if not the most important principles in golf is being able to vividly visualize the shot about to be played, down to the finest detail.

The ability to picture a successful shot before it is stuck is an integral part of most any sound modern teaching philosophy. Bob Rotella, noted sports psychologist to many tour players, even went as far as saying, "a golfer must lock her mind on the smallest possible target."[1] What I get out of that is you must forget about the water you're hitting over, the sand on either side of the green, and the trees on the way but instead focus on where you want the ball to go. Seeing the ball soar through the air and land softly on the green just a short putt away will properly set loose a creative mechanism in your brain that will help smooth out the bumps in your swing and help you find the green.

Focusing on where you don't want to go is a fatal mistake as the imagery of the mind only works on giving the viewer what it sees—and therefore if you picture the water, you get the water. The words "no water" do not process so it is simply translated as "water" by the brain so you must only visualize the positive outcomes.

The movie *7 Days in Utopia*[2] does a great job of impressing how a great golfer visualizes his shot. Robert Duvall plays a rusty older man of integrity that is a former golf professional turned rancher named Johnny. It is set in a small Texas town where a troubled young professional golfer named Luke Chisolm played by Lucas Black ends up finding his swing and finding his faith to return to the tour.

Duvall takes Black through a series of non-golf exercises similar to what Miyagi does with Daniel-san in the movie *The Karate Kid*.[3] One of those exercises involved setting up a canvas on the golf course about 130 yards away from the green but just a few yards behind a big oak tree. Lucas is puzzled why there are not any golf clubs but rather a canvas on an easel and watercolors. The wise old pro explains how it is necessary to paint the shot in your head before you can execute it.

Dr. David Cook, renowned sports psychologist and author of the book the movie was based on, tells the story for the inspiration of the scene of a time when his own golf professional the late Johnny Arreaga would yell "Picasso!" after hitting a great shot. When asked why he would yell that, Arreaga explained, "Every time you walk up to the tee you have a blank canvas in front of you, and you've got to paint the picture before you ever pull the club and hit the shot." Paraphrasing the story, you've got to see what you want the shot to look like very vividly before you can produce the shot. Dr. Cook said Johnny told him, "Whenever I hit a great shot all I am doing is signing the painting that I created in my mind."[4]

How does this play out in sales? You should visualize the results you want from the next cold call to the realtor or prospect. Visualize the audience applauding you for giving an excellent presentation. It is the visualization that helps to make it happen. It works for short-term goals as well as longer-term goals. If you are not where you want to be you can visualize yourself as a successful person. What type of car would you be driving? Where would you vacation? Where would you take your spouse out to dinner? What would you buy them for a birthday or anniversary?

Famed psychologist Maxwell Maltz in his book *Psycho Cybernetics*[5] states that the brain cannot differentiate between a vividly imagined scenario and the real thing.

Imagining these details is what allows your brain to see

these things as possible, probable, and then proven when you do them. Just having a goal is not enough. Just having a dream is not enough. It is necessary to be able to see how your life will be when you achieve that next level. It can't just be to make more money, it's got to be deeper. You've got to see what you would be doing with that money.

Let me give you an example. It's not just saying I would buy a brand new black BMW. You've got to paint the picture more precisely. Instead, imagine this. I see myself in that jet black 740i with the soft leather interior. You know the one that can pull itself out of the garage or the parking place by itself. I just use hand gestures to turn up the volume of the radio or just talk to the car as it has its own Alexa style Artificial Intelligence, so I can just ask where the next gas station is on the interstate or how far the next rest stop. Did I mention the wireless charging station and the new executive station in the back seat with the swing up table like on an airplane? How about the included tablet and vitality program to change the air conditioning setting, change the lighting or activate the built-in massage chair, it even has moonroof in the back seat executive station with ambient light patterns in the sunroof and surrounding area and even an ambient air package with 8 different fragrances to choose from.

I think you see what I mean. You just can't say I would buy a new car or new house. You have to make it more personal. You need to go out and test drive that car and start going to open houses with your spouse to pick out what you like and what your dream home would look like. You have to be emotionally invested in your dreams and your goals. Like I said before, your mind does not know the difference between a vividly imagined experience and the real thing, so to your subconscious you really are living that dream when you see it in such detail. And just like Johnny said, "Picasso!" you can start signing the painting and signing the checks to buy that new car and new house after you visualize it.

So, what happened to the young golfer with two holes to play on the windy day in West Texas? You can get the rest of the story and a lot of other great resources in relation to this book on my website: www.neversettleforpar.com

## 2 KEEP IN THE PRESENT

An average golfer can forget the first 9 hole and refocus on the last 9 if they played poorly on the front. A better golfer can leave the last hole in the past, but the best golfers play only in the present and don't think too far forward or in the past, they only address the shot they are playing. By staying in the present and focusing on what is most important now and having a vivid visualization of the shot before they hit it, they can bring the best outcome possible for their skill level at the time. That means that they realize that the time for practice was before the game day and little good can come by tinkering with their swing while in the game.

In sales being in the present is just as critical. To have thick skin and be able to leave the past behind you means not letting the last "no" keep you from making the next call.

Just as important is not getting ahead of yourself and getting too caught up in the emotion of closing a big deal before the work is all done. People can sense when you are too eager or too hungry to close the sale, so it's important not to count your chickens before they hatch.

It is also important to remember that goals are in concrete and plans are in sand. If you start off your month, your quarter or your year behind on your goal, realize that it is your plans to reach your goal that need to change and not the goal itself. When giving yourself a deadline to reach a goal, honor that. It may mean better time blocking, cutting out non-essential non-productive activities, bringing on an assistant or hiring a virtual assistant to do some of the non-money producing activities, but honor your goals. That is honoring a promise to yourself and to your family, you both deserve it!

## 3 BE YOURSELF

As a kid growing up in West Texas, golf does not seem like a likely sport of choice. I excelled at baseball as well, but I got very serious about golf around thirteen. I ended up giving up on all other sports to focus on golf at fourteen. I was in some ways too serious. I wanted to be good so bad that I often put too much pressure on myself when in tournaments and did not play up to my abilities.

I searched for years trying to find out why and it was not until I was in college that I found the answer. I had already finished a year of college golf as a freshman, playing not so successfully on an NAIA level golf team. Statistics say that less than 7% of golfers get to advance to the college level and even fewer than that are offered scholarships, so I guess I was lucky to make it that far. I expected more so I was discouraged at my performance, and so I transferred to a Texas Tech, a division one school nearby, where I knew I could get a better education. I continued to work in the golf business while in school at Texas Tech, so I continued to play and even played with some of the members of the Tech golf team in some weekend public tournaments. I had the reputation of someone with a great short game, so they wanted me to help out in scrambles and best ball tournaments. I always had a great time in these and played well. About that time, I realized that when I played my best golf was when I was joking around with my buddies, we would be poking fun at each other and talking trash. When I took myself too seriously or took the event too seriously, I fell out of my sweet spot and the pressure would often bring on poor performance. This proved itself true from taking too much time to prepare before a tournament round essentially "icing" myself by allowing the pressure to build before the competition began.

Now in the business world, I have embraced my history as a golf instructor, former golf professional, and a college golf coach as part of my unique selling proposition. It is what makes me different from my competition. I developed a majority of my business either with folks that I already knew from golf or others that they introduced me to and it has served me very well in the business world. Now you might be saying of course that is where your business came from after working in the industry for 15 years, but my point is deeper than that. I learned to make the two synergistic relationships. I did better at both because of the other and that was how I defined my niche. Learn more about that in Chapter 12.

# 4 OUTWORK YOUR COMPETITION

While I was at Texas Tech, I ran into a kid that I had played against in high school golf. I did not remember him but oh did he remember me. He said I was a stuck-up jerk when I was playing against him back when we were in high school. I was a little taken back by the comment, and he was shocked that I was so approachable now. I don't know if he thought I had grown out of it or what.

It was then that I realized how out of my normal behavior that I was acting when I was playing in competition back then. I apologized for how I treated him but he just kind of ignored it. He said he thought I was stuck up because I thought I was better than most of the other players out there, the fact was, I was better than them, not a better person but a better golfer. I was by no means being overly cocky or arrogant, but I was just being too serious and taking the game too serious and it came off as being stuck up. If I had been more my natural self, I would have been a better player and a much friendlier playing companion. I was confident but not cocky, golf just doesn't allow you to stay that way very long—golf, like life, has a way to continually keep you grounded and humble.

What I did learn from talking to him is that you are

going to get shot at when you are on top. Those that you are ahead of are going to try to drag you down and make up all kinds of excuses as to why they are not there and claim that you just got lucky when the fact is that winning on any level comes down to outworking the competition.

What he did not see behind the scenes was that I quit playing all other sports that I excelled at to focus all of my spare time on the one that I thought would get me to college for free and I spent four to five years playing and practicing virtually seven days a week four to six hours a day on weekdays and longer on the weekend in good weather and bad until I made it to the state golf tournament and placed in the top ten for our school division my senior year and I got my scholarship. Others called me lucky, anyone from my hometown who drove by the golf course those 4 years knew I paid for every cent of that scholarship on the cow pasture in Panhandle.

You've got to be your true authentic self to be truly successful in business. That can mean finding your niche in business or finding the part of the business that most fits your personality. You may enjoy being on stage and the center of attention so seminars and speaking may appeal to you. You may like being in the background doing behind the scenes marketing or another support role. All of these things can be an important part of the sales team. What can really move the needle in sales is when you find your why and find a way to fulfill that why that truly reflects your authentic self. Then you have a passion for what you are doing and enjoy how you are going to get it done. By doing a DISC profile (see page 29) with a Values assessment on yourself and other members of your team, you can find out what roles on the team they might be best suited for and all work more in unison toward a goal.

# 5 THE PRE-SWING ROUTINE

*Pre-Swing Routine-*

The Pre-Swing Routine is a sequence of precisely timed events that happen in order leading up to the execution of a golf shot. I say precisely timed because on the highest level you can actually put a stopwatch to a golf professional and see that the passage of time from when they start their routine to when they actually strike the ball can often be so precise that it's duplicated to within tenths of a second between two separate swings.

It really becomes an action on autopilot. It is similar to the type of training and repetition as is common in the military to allow certain actions to be repeated over and over again in an identical manner without conscious thought in order to be performed consistently while in the heat of the battle. The importance of the routine is to make the technical matters of the grip, aim, stance, and posture something that the mind does not have to occupy itself with so it can focus on the more important matter of visualizing the shot to be played.

*Scripting*

Within sales the use of practicing scripts and following

proven systems for the most important conversations in your sales cycle can serve the same purpose of having a sound swing routine. Knowing what you are going to say in the most critical moments allows some predictability in the process. It allows you to focus your perception, to study reactions, and to listen more actively so as to be able to go deeper into what the underlying needs are.

While actively listening, you are more likely to get to what their true needs are and to be able to overcome what could have been deflecting objection that was not truly the real obstacle in the way of a closed sale. I am not saying that you manipulate people but listen more attentively. I don't see the sales process as something that you do to someone, but more something that you do for someone. The best salespeople are those that search out needs and solve problems to add to the lives of their clients.

# 6 THE FUNDAMENTALS

*The Grip*

This is how the fingers are placed on the club. It is the only direct connection with the golf club that you have so it has to be right. It has been said that if you have a bad grip, you need a bad swing to compensate. The grip has the ability to impact the direction and curvature of the ball more than any other piece of the golf swing and changing it just a little can feel so awkward and produce very different results.

It is common for amateur golfers and even for some pros to continuously tweak their grip while over the ball in the pre-swing routine. That is something not to be recommended especially if it is in relation to indecision as it can lead to negative thoughts and inhibit a clear mental image of the shot about to be played. Tour pro Sergio Garcia got into a habit of constantly gripping and re-gripping the club repeatedly during his waggle and his routine. He got so bad during the early 2000s that some spectators were counting his grip adjustments and got to numbers up into the thirties on some swings. You want to place the hands on the club and then forget it. It should be something that is automatic.

*Verbiage*

I equate the grip to your delivery or your verbiage in sales. That is why scripting can be so vital in making sure that you get the desired message across. You have to know what you are planning on saying at each stage of the sales cycle and test different scripts for the intended result being careful to always keep the spirit of the script but to change it enough to fit your words and your delivery style.

I see the grip can also be like your style or your brand. Once settled into your sweet spot you should own it, get comfortable with it, and wear it like a medal. It is what differentiates you from others.

*AIM*

Aim seems pretty clear. What are you aiming for? Harvey Penick, one of golf's great instructors, in his *Little Red Book* said to "take dead aim."[6] Bob Rotella a modern golf sports psychologist in one of his "Rotella's Rules" stated that a golfer must "lock his or her eyes on the smallest possible target."[7] That is, aim at what you see in your mind's eye of the target.

One of the tricks that golf course architects use is to narrow your focus as you look from the tee to the green and to limit your vision to prevent you from seeing the trouble that lies just out of sight when looking from the tee box. That is why my college golf coach would often have us walk the golf course in reverse from the eighteenth green to the eighteen tee and on backward because you would get a different perspective on the golf course. Things that the architect would try to hide from you would become apparent allowing you to easily see where the best place to play the approach while standing on the green looking back, the best angle to come into the green from, and the best placement off of the tee while standing in the fairway looking back at the tee box.

*Goal Setting*

In life and sales, determining where you're aimed means setting your goals. I don't have any idea where this originated from to give due credit, but I have heard this from many sources about goals. They should be SMARTER.

- **S**pecific
- **M**easurable
- **A**ttainable
- **R**elevant
- **T**ime Bound
- **E**xecuted (as quickly as possible)
- w**R**itten

*Specific* means that you have exact amounts of what it is you want to achieve. Just as with visualization, vague or unclear goals leave too much up to chance or doubt. The more specific and detailes they are, the more likely you will be able to see your way to achieving them.

*Measurable* – You have to be able to know if you've hit the mark or not so you know when you're on track or how much you need to step it up and when to celebrate your successes.

*Attainable* – If you set goals that are too far out of your reach they may seem unrealistic and only discourage you when you are not seeing meaningful progress toward them; however, setting goals that are so low as to be attained with little effort does not really feel like a win. There needs to be the right balance of difficulty yet achievability. It should require some real effort to attain, but with that right amount of effort, there should be a tangible win waiting on the other side.

*Relevant* – Your goals need to be relevant to what your core values are and what you really want to achieve because otherwise, you will find yourself reaching them only to find little satisfaction when you realize that you are farther away from what it is that you get real satisfaction from.

*Time Bound* – Any goal without a time frame is no goal at all. It is simply a dream. If there is no sense of urgency, it tells the mind that it is really not important to you.

*Executed immediately* – Okay, I added these last two to the normal SMART to make it SMARTER, but that is because you are 85% more likely to get something accomplished if you start implementing it within twenty-four hours of setting the goal.

*wRitten* – Yes it has to be written down. It can't be specific without being written and there needs to be a record so you can consult back to it and revisit it to keep it fresh. I recommend posting a copy on your bathroom mirror, at your desk at work, as your desktop screensaver or anywhere else where you will have to see them on a regular basis so you are constantly reminded of them.

You have to start with the goal and then work it backward to determine the activity it takes to get it. For example, a mortgage broker with an average loan size of $200,000 that wants to do $10MM in sales in a year needs to have fifty transactions. If he has a 75% submission to close ratio then he needs sixty-seven submissions to close fifty, if he has a 25% application to submission ratio, then he needs to take 268 applications in order to get sixty-seven submissions. If he has an average one application per two calls, then he needs to make 536 calls to get the necessary number of applications and so forth.

*Stance – Posture*

Golf is played from a fairly standard "athletic ready" position. It is similar to the stance that a tennis player would take preparing for a return of serve or a baseball fielder when preparing for the pitch to be delivered. Poor posture results in poor balance which means an out of time and out of control swing.

Having the correct posture in sales is akin to having the right frame of mind and the right attitude before going into the sales arena. It is necessary to be confident and poised but not so much as to come off as arrogant or greedy.

# 7 ALIGNMENT AND YOUR WHY

Alignment which is the orientation of the body in relation to the direction the player intends the ball travel. This often-overlooked part of the golf set up is the most prominent cause of a good player developing a faulty swing.

Good golfers have a natural athletic ability that allows them to have a repetitive, balanced, graceful motion that because of the rhythm and balance it masks just how fast the club is actually moving. They can repeat the motion over and over again with amazing accuracy, but if they get just a few degrees out of alignment it can cause the ball to miss the fairway or the green and end up in the water, sand or even out of bounds. The player, not realizing that he is misaligned starts messing with an otherwise sound golf swing in order to get the ball back on line and can develop some really bad habits that disrupt what was a very sound motion turning it into an out of balance and out of rhythm lashing at the golf ball.

In sales, you've got to have goals and know what it takes to get there. You can't allow yourself to get off track of your goal or to venture out of your sweet spot. That is where having a really good WHY comes in.

There are always going to be obstacles and setbacks in golf, sales, and life for that matter. No one has ever shot 18 in golf. Money and the pursuit of a perfect score alone will not serve as sufficient motivation when things are at their worst, so you have to have a bigger reason that will keep you going even when you don't feel like it.

*Finding Your WHY?*

If you have not ever done this exercise before do it now. You can practice it with a friend or your spouse or with a peer at work. This is an adaptation from the 5 Golden Questions by Allan Pease in his book *The Questions are the Answers*.[8]

- What is your number one priority in life? What is your big WHY?

- *Why did you choose that?*

- Why is that important is it to you? (This questions asks, "Tell me again why you chose that and for what reason?")

- What would be the consequences of not achieving that? (Or "what would happen to you if you did not achieve that?")

- Does that bother you? (This makes them get emotional about their reason)

- How is it going? (If they're honest this is where they

let you know where their pain is)

- Do you have a 3-5 year 5-10 year plan to get you there? (This tests the water to see how their current planning is going to see if they are where the opportunity is)

You can use this process to more clearly focus on what your why is to keep you connected to your core values. Some folks may try to short circuit the process and say they work for money, for those, you need to ask yourself what do you want the money for? Once you've gone 3 or four levels deeper on asking why on that you will get to a core value.

You can also use this process to help dive down into what a prospect values so you can more clearly see what problems that they might have and how to frame your solution in terms of what they truly value.

In this situation, your response is repeating back the "why" to get to the third level. For example if a Realtor told you his highest priority was having a more predictable process (why?) so he could make more money in less time (why?) to spend more time with his or her family you could say, "That is exactly what our business model is designed to do. To allow you to (inserting their why) provide your clients with a more predictable process, ensuring a timely closing and the ability to do more transactions and make more money with less staff freeing up time to enjoy with your family. Now it is their reason, it is not yours. Even if you were lucky enough to guess their reason and you told them what you could do for them before they told you what was important to them, they would most likely raise objections because it was you who supplied the reason not them. Now they can't take away their why since they are the ones that supplied it.

This progression of questioning if answered sincerely gets to a person's core reasons for doing what they do. It can be adapted to a lot of situations with a little tweaking, but its real power is in its open-ended nature. When you find out what it is that really motivates people, you don't have to tell them the reasons to do business with you, you just have to find out what you can do to help them.

You could write a whole book about finding your why, and in fact several people have. Instead of trying to exhaust the subject I'd rather refer you to someone who has done just that, Simon Sinek. His book *Start with Why* and his work on the subject in my opinion is the best that you can find. You can also visit his website also titled www.startwithwhy.com for some free videos and resources on the subject.

# 8 THE WAGGLE

The waggle is the slow back and forth motion of the club that starts the swing going. It is a tension breaker that gives the muscles a little preview of the dynamic weight of the club and a feel of the swing to help prevent the jerkiness that often results from trying to start the club from a dead stop. When I want to try and change a player's swing, the waggle is often where I start.

The reason is that it is the last motion that is semi-conscious before the player moves into the sequence that is his or her naturally repetitive golf swing. It is a sort of starting point where we can inject some conscious intervention before the unconscious mind takes over. We'll cover more on that later. Now I am not saying that all swings are good because they are repetitive, they are just consistent meaning they repeat the same mistakes. I'd say a lot of us do the same thing because we are resistant to change.

The waggle also serves as a tempo setter and is notably the official start of the progression of a precisely timed and mostly involuntary or unconscious motion that can dictate the rest of the swing. It is the first move made before the actual golf swing is taken, but it is really still a part of the swing.

The waggle is what sets the pace and provides a preview of the swing, by comparison, in sales it is where you set the tone and point of the meeting. It is where you give insight to your prospect as to what the purpose of the meeting is.

In order to set a proper tone, "the waggle" should be the things you do to relax yourself before a potentially high impact activity. It's taking a deep breath, saying some affirmations, and the pre-meeting self-talk you give yourself before you pick up the phone or meet with someone in person. This is where you take the specific outcome that you want to come from the activity and set the tone as to how you want to come across to your client or prospect.

Setting the correct tone with prospects or potential clients means the right tone of voice, the right level of expectations, and being able to relay that in a way that they are receptive to. Picking up on their personality, style, and delivering in a manner that is consistent with their style is a good way to strengthen your chances. By style I am referring to their DISC profile. If you have never heard of this, I will provide some background. The DISC Model of Behavior was introduced by William Moulton Marston, a physiological psychologist with a Ph.D. from Harvard.

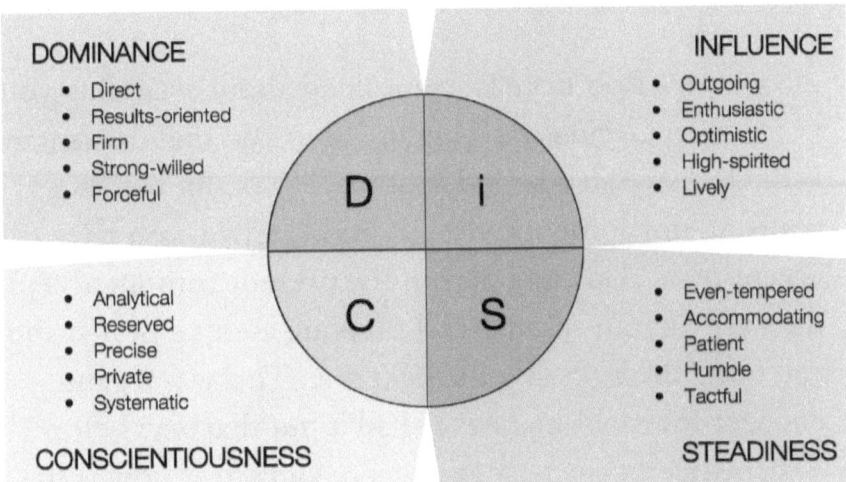

All of us are some mixture of the above categories but tend to favor one over the others. Knowing what their tendencies are and what yours are will help you to communicate better. D's are direct and to the point; they need bullet points. I's are outgoing and enthusiastic; they seek fun. S's are grounded and steady they seek security and avoid confrontation. Finally, I's are analytical and need the details.

I am not going to provide an exhaustive review of DISC but suffice it to say it would serve you well if you had a DISC assessment done for you and your team, and you read a book or two about it to put the concepts into practice. Dr. Robert Rohm wrote one of the first books on the subject and he is one of the more respected experts on the subject. I would recommend Dr. Rohm's *Positive Personality Profiles* but and he has written several others since it was first published in 1993 and updated in 2000.[9]

*Acceptance* – Bob Rotella in speaking about accepting your last shot in *Golf is not a Game of Perfect* said that "acceptance is the last step in a sound routine."[10] You hit the shot yourself, not someone else, so good or bad, you have to accept that. You can't play in the present without accepting the past. If your mind is still thinking about a blown shot, it can't be fully assessing the next one. This was a game changer for me. I had never had it put that way before. Acceptance of the past and where you are at now is the key to the future. It allows you to control what you can control because no one can change the past, but they can redirect their thinking toward a better future.

I would say this is a direct correlation to sales rejection or challenges in life. We have all had setbacks and faced critical times when it just seems like nothing is going our way and it is so easy to play the blame game and to feel sorry for ourselves or angry at others. The issue with that is, it does nothing to change our situation or to help navigate the path out of it. It only serves to dig ourselves deeper into the pit of misery and effectively bury ourselves in our own losses.

In order to right the ship we have to accept that we played a part in getting ourselves there in the first place. Also, it is important to note that changing a golf swing or a life takes aligning yourself correctly and working on the right things for a long enough time to start seeing results. There is no magic pill that automatically turns an inconsistent golf swing into a consistent one. It often takes just as long to play yourself out of a big slump as it took you to dig yourself into it and the same is true in life. You must do a self-assessment, realize that where you are is not where you want to be, and map out the course to where you want to be. And it wouldn't hurt to hire a coach, a trusted advisor who has been in your shoes. They are someone who can take an objective look at where you are and help point you in a better direction and avoid some of the obstacles that their years of experience can help you avoid.

# 9 CADDIES AND COACHES

Golf can often seem like a very lonely sport. I remember some of my first tournaments as a college golfer playing at a much higher level of competition than I ever had before and everyone there had the potential to beat me on any given day. It was a very lonely experience when I did not know anyone that I was playing against, none of them knew me, and they all could play some great golf. Needless to say, I had some not so great starts playing college golf. At the college level, there were no caddies. College golf tournaments are often hundreds of miles apart and across multiple states continuing for 3 or 4 days at a time so it was not practical for most parents to try and travel to most events so there were few parents walking around watching kids play.

It was very isolating. What I really needed was a caddy. Caddies were not allowed on the college level, but they were in some of the higher level junior golf competitions that I played in before college and after college. A caddy is someone to be there with you to remind you of past successes, speak truth and confidence to you, help you walk through the decisions, keep you grounded and calm, to be a friend when everyone else is a competitor.

A good coach knows when to be supportive and when to push. They know your personality and know how to get the best out of you. After the first round of my second college tournament did not go so well, my coach came up to me when no one else was around. Coach Richardson was a big guy, a former college football player and also a coach on the football team; he knew what he was doing as a coach. He was both stern and funny and had a ton of one-liners he got from a life in sports both playing and coaching and being around the characters.

He once compared one of our golfers to a "walking one iron" as he was a taller skinny kid without much meat on his bones. Coach pulled me aside and said, "What are you doing out there Conway?" I looked at him quizzically. He continued, "Why are you playing like that? You've got more talent than anyone out here, but you're not playing up to your ability." Those words were exactly what I needed. I'm sure after years of coaching athletes he was aware that I was feeling the pressure of being the new kid on the team and the much higher level of competition that I was playing in. I stepped up the next round and shot the third best round of the tournament to pass more than half of the field after the first round. I didn't finish in the top ten, but I finally got in a round of golf that I could be proud of and more in line with how I had played back in high school when I was a big fish in a small pond.

Have you ever felt like that in the sales world? I know the feeling and it was exactly the same, anxious, nervous, isolated and on edge sensation. Who can be there to help you navigate this jungle? I don't know when coaching became commonplace in sales but let me tell you it has definitely had an impact in the last five to ten years. Their job is not the same as that of your manager or your boss, they are not your assistant or your buddy. They are your mentor, your psychologist, your pastor, your trusted advisor, your sounding board, your rudder, and your biggest fan.

You chose to work with them instead of working for them like a boss. The relationship with a good coach is so much more. They are there to celebrate your victories with you, pick you up when you lose, plan your approach to the game, share best practices, shed light in the dark and most of all to be the greatest fan and believer in you when you might not believe in yourself. Why wouldn't someone want one?

The purpose they serve is like a good accountant or financial planner, although they may come at a cost, the service they provide more than pays for itself. Not only does a good coach often up your income but more importantly for many, they give perspective and add balance to your life giving a boost not just to your finances, but to all the roles you play in your life.

## 10 LIFE ON TOUR ~ THE HOME TEAM

As I ventured into the world of golf as a profession, perhaps the number one reason I was able to do that is I had parents that let my brother and I choose our own paths and a spouse that was supportive of me while I was in the profession. My brother was a talented musician and wanted to pursue a career in music as much as I was drawn to golf. Now, most parents would have tried to redirect us to a more practical pursuit like being a business professional, but that was not our parents. They gave us enough room to make our own way, and supported us whatever our choices were, even when I changed paths a few times from wanting to go to law school and being in politics, then reverting back to golf as a profession. They always believed in me, even when things were hard and not going my way, which encouraged me and helped me to belive in myself,

For a touring golf professional, someone had to be responsible for keeping the home fire burning. Although I played in some professional events, I never played as a touring professional on the road every week trying to make the cut. I have had friends and students that played on tour as well as some that caddied and I know from their stories how tough that was. The dream of playing golf on tour would not have been possible if it was not for their spouses' sacrifice to take care of business at home, like taking care of the house and children for weeks or even months at a time while the pro was out on tour for the season. One wife that I know even packed up bags and went on the road too, and served as spouse, relief car driver, and caddy. That takes a lot of guts and a lot of trust in each other to risk it all together.

A life in sales is no easy matter and it seems like it takes a toll on everyone in the family, so it is crucial to have all members of the family playing a supportive role. I tried to make sure that my wife knew what my goals were so that she could both help keep me accountable and also encourage me on the way. She knew that a victory in a 100% commission industry often had rewards in it that the whole family could share in like great vacations, home additions, and new cars!

It is also important to realize the sacrifice that your family makes to allow you to do what it is that you love. Honor their sacrifice by being there for the most important events in their lives like the big games and dance auditions, not forgetting your wife's birthday and your anniversary. It can mean just simply sitting on the floor to play cars or trains with your son, having a tea party with your daughter, or when they are older taking time after work to throw the ball with them or just playing in the yard on nice days. That is one of the biggest benefits of the flexibility a well-balanced sales career can provide.

## 11 FOCUS IN AND FOCUS OUT

When I was in competitive golf in high school and college and was in my super focused mode, it was because I was very focused on winning and playing well. A few times I was able to stay in this mode for a full four to six hour round of golf, but I would get tremendous headaches and be exhausted after playing. During competition, if you are too caught up in what you want and not paying enough attention to the process, you can get overly concerned with results and lose sight of what you are doing in the present.

Later I learned a better method that allowed me to be focused right before the shot when I really needed it and then to go back to my normal more relaxed and funny sarcastic self after the shot. I call it "playing in your own skin". I could be serious and focused in short spurts without expending all of that mental energy when it was not needed. As a result of this shift, I was much more comfortable and happy while playing and I played more freely and much better in competition.

In the world of business and sales, it is important to stay in the present and not get too far ahead of yourself. If you get overly focused on the goal and don't pay enough attention to the process, you can become too results driven and start missing important parts of the sales cycle. I have seen good salespeople sell themselves right out of a deal when they got too focused on closing the sale to pay attention to non-verbal clues, and some verbal ones that the sale prospect was all ready to buy. One of my mentors used to say "stop drilling you've already struck oil!" Remember that good salespeople are trying to find a need, which means to ask questions and then to listen. Listen and pay attention to the verbal and the non-verbal cues of your prospects and let them guide you to your next step in determining a need.

Don't forget to give yourself some downtime. If you need to do a 4-hour block of calling, it is important to put a sign on the door that you are in sales dialing mode and do not disturb. It is also important to give yourself a short break of 5 to 10 minutes every hour or two to let your brain cool the engine a bit, get a drink of water or stretch your legs but then put the sign back up and get right back to it. Focusing too intently for too long of a period of time can cause burnout and cause your intensity and mental acuity to drop substantially if it is maintained for too long.

The same can be said of working too much without a day off or taking a decent vacation where you were not involved with work at all. I know in sales that can be tricky if you have clients in the sales cycle where your paycheck depends on them closing, but that is where it is paramount that you have a team, a backup or a partner or peer that can cover for you when you are out, and you can exchange the favor when they are taking time off.

It is vital to your family that you take some exclusive time with them without urgent phone calls, constantly staring down at your phone texting or returning messages and not taking time just to be in the moment fully with your loved ones. They are most likely what you are working for to begin with so do yourself a favor and work out a coverage plan with your boss, a peer or your team before things get too busy and harder to implement one.

## 12 FIND YOUR NICHE

I guess the biggest lesson I got out of what my parents did for me was they allowed me to find my own niche in life. I have had several of my sales managers say that the secret to success is finding your niche or your unique sales proposition. I think I have always known it, but it took a little time to hone.

Some sales folks will tell you that they have great service. I'll tell you that you better or you will be out of business, so I don't consider that unique. Others will tell you that they have great pricing and I think that is a one-way ticket to the poor house. Someone can and will always be willing to beat your price, so that is not the way to differentiate yourself unless you want to be bankrupt. What you have to figure out is what is it that makes you unique that no one else can copy? What is your brand? Mine was golf.

I did an exercise some eight or nine years ago where I traced all of my sales for the last five to ten years in the business trying to source where all of the business came from. Being that I was in the golf industry in Nashville for the first eight to ten years after moving there from West Texas, the majority of my sphere of influence came from golf. My brother, who had moved to Nashville a few years earlier to pursue a music career also introduced me to quite a few folks in the music business. I found that over 33% of my business was folks that I had met through golf and over 66% were relationships that were one level of separation from a golf relationship. I was thinking of getting away from golf, but after I did that analysis, I found out that what I really needed to do was to embrace the symbiotic relationship that golf had played in my business.

In retrospect, there were few demographic groups that could have served me better as I was trying to find middle to upper-income buyers, realtors or affinity partners to refer business to me. We spoke a similar language, I knew they were largely dedicated and honest people, they had higher than average incomes, they embraced a challenge and were hard workers. I knew all of that about them simply by knowing that they were dedicated golfers. I also knew that few would turn down an opportunity to meet with me knowing my background and my knowing they loved to play golf. A legendary Texas golf instructor from Austin Country Club wrote a book that sums it all up in its title, *And if you play golf, you're my friend.*[11]

## 13 PRACTICE WITH PURPOSE

A great player always has a specific intent when he is working on his game. He never goes to the practice facility just to practice and you should never go into a meeting just to meet. You should always have a specific intent and goal for every meeting. It may have multiple purposes like a first meeting with a prospective referral partner is most likely to assess their business, determine their needs and to see if there is a fit. Do your research so you know a little about them before you go into the meeting. Social media sites liked Facebook and LinkedIn are your biggest asset when you are searching for new referral partners. They can give you a gold mine of data to help you figure out their interests, learn about their family and what type of music they like to hear and more.

*Practice* – Find something that you love and do it.

My golf youth was spent on a nine hole flatland cow pasture golf course called Panhandle Country Club in the Texas Panhandle. It was a simple short nine hole course with a small practice putting green, no driving range and nine holes. Suffice it to say I did not do a lot of practicing my full shots. It was too much work when you had to chase down your own golf balls, so when I was not playing I learned to love to practice the short game.

After school was out at 3:45, I would head straight to the golf course where I played nine holes. Then I spent the rest of the day, and sometimes into the night, under the single street light that was set in the middle of the practice green, chipping and putting, and it was a good thing. I really never was a great ball striker, so I needed to lean on my strengths to take me to the next level.

*If it wasn't hard, I wouldn't like it!* –Hard things offer their own Reward.

My brother Gary watched one of the local club champions Gary B. working on hitting a low shot into the wind in the little area that we had where you could hit 150 to 200-yard shots for practice alongside the first fairway. Gary B. was one of the top two or three players because he was one of the top two or three hardest workers on his golf game. It was even more hard work because we did not have a driving range so after you hit the balls you had to retrieve them in order to hit them again. My brother asked him, "Gary why do you work so hard at this game? Isn't that a lot of work that you are putting in for just a game?" and Gary B. responded, "You know what Gary, if it wasn't hard I wouldn't like it."

Those words struck a chord with my brother. It had enough of an impact on him that he shared it with me and to this day over thirty years later I still remember it.

Hard things attract a certain kind of person, someone who is not afraid of a challenge. In fact they thrive when faced with difficult situations, it makes them focus in on the most important things and grind in order to win. If you are that kind of a person, there is no end to the world of challenging work that is out there that you can find rewarding both psychologically and finically. After all, most of your harder professions pay higher returns. You just have to find the one that fits your personality and either learn to love it or find the part of it you love and set up systems or find someone else to do the rest.

## 14 GIVING UP CONTROL

The golf swing has often been described as giving up control to gain control. No good shot comes from trying to force it to happen or over think it. Only bad things happen to the natural flowing motion of swings when mechanical thoughts sweep and take away the mind and body's natural creative mechanisms to perfectly time such a complex and precise motion. Just a few degrees of rotation of the head of a driver moving at 100 miles per hour can careen the ball yards off line from the middle of the intended fairway deep into the woods or the water. The swing itself is supposed to be graceful and powerful like a pair of professional dancers spinning together in time without thought and just losing themselves in the motion.

For someone in a sales career that form of giving up control to gain control can only be achieved when they have brought on an assistant because there are far too many intricacies of the business that have to be addressed that are outside of the skill sets of just one person. The typical top producer in sales is someone without great attention to detail. They are a "D" type personality which means they are dominant doers and action takers.

They need someone else to manage the minutia of the

sales process and often lack the strength of will or faith to be able to trust someone else to do the job, but they must. Here is where they must give up control in order to gain control because there is no top producer who does it alone. The challenge is, how do you know what tasks you should keep and which ones you can offload to an assistant or a system?

It all starts with a list. First, brainstorm with a colleague or two about all of the things that you have to do in your role from the most mundane like checking email and returning phone calls to sending thank you notes to making sales call. Be as exhaustive on this list as you can so as to be sure that you have everything that you do listed. If you miss a couple you can always come back. It might help to break them down into broad categories like administrative duties, marketing duties, sales duties, etcetera, and then list all of the items below them. I have included a sample for someone in the mortgage industry labeled, "The Chopping Block" on my website www.coachwithwade.com/bookresources

Next, if I were to make you pick JUST ONE activity and tell you that is the only activity that you could do for your business for the next two weeks straight, what would that activity be? Be serious and don't pick something general like sales, it must be more specific like face to face appointments with realtors or making phone calls to top producing agents. Once you have that, you know what your top priority in business most likely is. This one activity should probably be the one thing that moves the needle the most forward for you and you need to spend the majority of your time doing it.

After you have picked that one activity, what is the next single activity that you would add to it that you would do if you could only do two things? Progress like this until you have a list of all of the things that you and only you could do for you and you should have a list of the top three to five things that are the biggest money producing activities for your business and the best use of YOUR time. Now that you have that you know what your job is and it is now time to figure out who is going to do the rest of the stuff on your list. Here are the steps in order.

1. Make a list of all you do.
2. Pick out the activities that only you could do.
3. Delegate the rest to other people or create a system to do it for you.

So where do you find someone to hire to do these things for you? I highly recommend that you reach out to your friends and colleagues in your business. Somewhere out there is someone in sales that does not really have the personality profile to be the rainmaker but that would be very comfortable and successful being the support team to cut and clean what you bring home from the hunt. I've even included a sample business ad for a support person at my website www.coachwithwade.com/bookresources

I recommend trying to bring someone in that already has a mortgage license and has a two year or more track record of some level of production as your loan officer's assistant otherwise your business will end up slowing down for months in order to try and train them. If there is someone else within your company that is on commission but struggling and knows the process but is just not a good rainmaker, they could be a great fit.

Most importantly before you hire them, first make sure they meet the experience required above and second make sure they fit the DISC profile of an assistant.

Below is an excerpt from Jay Niblick (how golf appropriate) from WizeHire.com They are an excellent resource for hiring the right fit for all professions. You can get DISC reports at their website and also free job listing templates for positions that you need to fill listed by position with the targeted DISC profiles needed for each role.

- Moderate to low level of the D dimension in the DISC profile, which helps him or her make more deliberate and careful decisions with details and tasks.
- Moderately high I dimensional scores, which makes him or her personable extroverts who work well with a wide variety of people.
- High levels in the S dimension, which contributes to him or her being great stabilizers, consistent and reliable.

- High levels of the C dimension, which makes him or her bulldogs for details, neurotic for accuracy and sticklers for making sure everything is done by the book.
- From a motivational standpoint, exceptional administrative assistants are:
- Driven by high levels of altruism, and sincerely like making sure everyone is well taken care of and supported.
- Enjoy working inside the lines where there are lots of regulations, policies, rules and structure.
- Always hungry for new knowledge or new ways of delivering even more efficient results.

Niblick, Jay (Nov. 18, 2016) *What Makes a Successful Real Estate Assistant* retrieved from:
https://wizehire.com/blog/great-real-estate-executive/#gs.YoLm6tc

## 15 PLAY IT WHERE IT LIES ~ INTEGRITY

Golf is the only sport that I know of where players call a penalty on themselves. Only at the highest levels of professional competition are there officials on every hole to officiate and call penalties, the rest of the time it is up to the players to police themselves. There is no more famous example in the game than that of Bobby Jones in the 1925 US Open.

There is a true story about the great Bobby Jones, legendary amateur golfer and designer of Augusta Country Club, the famed club where The Master's tournament resides and a member of the greatest generation. In the 1925 US Open, Jones called a penalty on himself for unintentionally moving a ball while setting up for a shot.

His competitor and play companions did not see it, no one in the crowd saw it, and yet he still assessed the penalty on himself as he was adamant that he had caused the ball to move. The one-shot penalty ended up costing him the win as he ended in a tie with another golfer and it went to a playoff which Jones lost. After being praised for his act of honor by the press after the match, Jones quipped, "You may as well praise me for not robbing banks."[12] The only way that he knew to play was with honesty and integrity.

In business, being honest and acting with integrity should be the norm, but that is not always the case in today's cutthroat world of "me first." Nevertheless, integrity matters. Social media and instant news over the web have made the business environment so public and government regulations so tight that no company can afford to employ a salesman who would say anything or do anything just to get the sale. Such a person is a huge liability and not an asset to a company.

George Akerlof was the winner of the 2001 Nobel Peace Prize for Economics and Sciences for his work titled *The Market for Lemons* where he points out that lack of integrity was one of the factors that increase a buyer's perception of risk. Akerlof said, "Dishonest dealings tend to drive honest dealings out of the market. The cost of dishonesty, therefore, lies not only in the amount by which the purchaser is cheated; the cost also must include the loss incurred from driving legitimate business out of existence."[13] Essentially that lack of integrity in selling costs both buyers and sellers.

I definitely saw this before the more stringent regulation in the mortgage industry but still see it some today where online lead sellers posing as mortgage lenders are advertising rates well below market without clearly identifying that there are in fact other costs to get that rate like costly buydowns, or the product is not clearly disclosed as a more risky adjustable rate loan. I lost business to folks using these shady business tactics causing me to appear as a costlier option. Of course, when the truth came out at time of application or in the old days at closing, the buyer would be furious and the cost was a loss of trust in not just the salesman but the industry. That exemplifies why it is even more important to distance yourself and your business from anyone or anything that even might be perceived to be shady or deceptive. In the end, it will serve you and your business best to always be honest with folks and treat them with integrity.

## 16 CONFIDENCE

It's impossible to play good golf without having confidence. You should have confidence in yourself, confidence in your ability to execute any given shot and confidence that you are able to win.

I remember a particular match I was playing in that if I won or placed second it would advance me to the state tournament. Tournaments usually pair the leaders together so that the leader, the guy in second that was up on me a few shots, and I were playing together in the last group. I knew that I at least had to beat the guy in second and since I was a little behind I figured that I needed to shoot seventy-two or better to win and I needed to play the last three holes at two or three under par, but my driving had been off that day. I wasn't going to let that break my confidence as I was just one or two over par and I had been playing well all day.

The last three holes are a couple of straightforward par fours and then a longer uphill par five with trees guarding both sides of the fairway. I had been having problems hooking my tee ball and long irons, so I had been playing it safe off of the tee. After making a straightforward two-putt par on sixteen, I blocked my drive right on seventeen trying to avoid the dreaded hook. I had about 120 yards in but had to basically punch the ball under the trees that lined the right side to get to the green.

I executed a pretty good shot that just made the front of the green but had at least thirty feet for birdie. A birdie on seventeen and one on eighteen or an eagle on eighteen would most likely sew it up for me, so I was focused on that putt knowing if I made it I had a good chance of the birdie on the par five last hole. I lined it up and visualized the shot and pulled the trigger. It rolled as true as a chalk line straight in the cup. I gave it a fist pump, but there was no time to celebrate as I still faced a tricky tee shot on eighteen.

Knowing I needed to get off the tee well, I took a risk with the driver, but it got caught in the upper branches of a tree on the right side forcing me to punch it out to the fairway. It was in a decent spot in the left center of the fairway, but the problem was, the way that I was hooking my longer shots I would have to take the approach shot up over the trees on the right and let it drawback in from over 220 yards out in order to get it to go up the steep hill and still get back to the green. I can still picture that two-iron shot in my head from thirty years ago soaring out over the tree line and then curving smoothly back down and around to land on the green and roll just ten or fifteen feet above the cup. Let me tell you there was no chance I could have executed that shot without first seeing it so clearly in my head and then trusting that I could pull it off.

I was still faced with a slick, tricky little downhill putt for the birdie. I was last to putt as I was closest to the hole.

After the round, my coach, Coach Cox, came up to me and gave me a high five and quick man-hug in congratulations. He told me you should have seen that look that I gave my fellow competitor as soon as the putt dropped. He said the look in my eye was pure triumph, conviction, and confidence almost as if I had willed the putt to drop. As it turned out, that putt won me the trip to the state tournament as I had just edged my competitor out of a second place finish and the top two finishers got to proceed to state.

When you step into the sales arena, you have to know that you can win. You have to have the expectation that your product and service provides a great benefit for your clients. You have to be able to transfer that expectancy and conviction to them in your demeanor, your confidence, your words, and your tone. If you don't believe in yourself and your product, no one else will.

People are drawn toward those that exude confidence and integrity there is a void of it today. Especially missing is the humble, sincere type of confidence you see in a character like Jimmy Stewart played in *Mr. Smith Goes to Washington*. If you have not seen it do yourself a favor and go watch it with your spouse this weekend. Watch the scene where he addresses Congress, it's a classic.

## DON'T BEAT YOURSELF

There are plenty of competitors in the world of sales. As my former college golf coach says, "there are 120 other players out here today more than happy to whip you, you don't have to beat yourself." Don't look at a sale as taking advantage of someone. You are filling a need. Someone else could sell to them, and they may not be as honest as you and their product may be inferior so do *them* a favor and fill their need and get them off the market.

Golf and sales are two of the most demanding pursuits and they tend to attract people strong in character. They are hard enough on their own without you beating yourself up after having a bad day or getting a rejection.

The best definition of sales I know is that you are identifying a need and offering a solution that fits. Think about it like offering someone a cookie. It wouldn't bother you if someone declined, after all, some folks don't like cookies! Don't take yourself too seriously. We've all had bad days so give yourself permission to laugh at yourself now and then. It can be refreshing.

## THE 19^TH HOLE ~ CONCLUSION

I hope you've gotten some value out of this book and it has served to give you light and direction to help you if you are new to the field. Or if you are a veteran struggling to get to the next level, I pray it helps you find that youthful exuberance that may have been missing from your life.

I know the sales world has definitely been a blessing to me and my family over the last fifteen years since I ventured out of golf as my career but still found a way to benefit from my experiences in the industry and around the great people that play the game.

Additionally, I hope that what you got out of this book helps you to challenge traditional sales models of dialing for dollars and cold calling through the phone book and look deeper at what it takes to develop more meaningful relationships with those that you partner with, those you work with, those whose need your goods or service.

I hope you can see sales fills a vital role by finding and fulfilling those needs and providing great products and services to those you serve.

Finally, I pray that you find your calling in life and that you someday have the experience of having a full and rewarding life serving a greater purpose than yourself, and not making money just for the sake of making it.

May you give freely of your time and resources to those

you love and others not because of what you can get out of it but because you want to sew blessings into their lives and may they return that love to you so that you can truly live a blessed life.

God Bless.

Fairways and Greens,
Wade

# BIBLIOGRAPHY

1. Rotella, Dr. Bob *Golf is not a Game of Perfect* Simon and Schuster 1995 Print
2. Berman, Michael A (Producer) Russell, Mathew Dean (Director) (2011) *7 Days in Utopia* [Motion Picture] U.S. Box Office Mojo based on the book by Dr David Cook
    a. Cook, David L 2009 *Golf's Sacred Journey: Seven Days at the Links of Utopia.* Zondervan 2009 Print
3. Weintraub, Jerry (Producer) Avildsen, John G (Director) *The Karate Kid* [Motion Picture] U.S. Delphi II Productions 1984
4. Cook, Dr. Davis *The Psychology of Tournament Golf* Sacred Journey Stories 2014 Print
5. Maltz, Maxwell *Psycho-Cybernetics* Simon and Schuster 1960 Print
6. Penick, Harvey with Shrake, Bud *Harvey Penick's Little Red Book: Lessons and Teachings from a Lifetime in Golf* Simon and Schuster 1992 Print
7. Rotella (ibid) *Golf is Not a Game of Perfect*
8. Pease, Alan *Questions are the Answers* Manjul Publishing House 2008 Print
9. Rohm, Dr. Robert *Positive Personality Profiles* 4th Ed. Personality Insights Inc 1994 Print
10. Rotella (ibid) *Golf is Not a Game of Perfect*
11. Penick, Harvey with Shrake, Bud *And if you Play Golf, You're My Friend* Fireside Books Simon and Schuster 1999 Print
12. Excerpt from the *Life and Times of Bobby Jones* by Sidney L. Matthew Sleeping Bear Press, 1995, Page 75
13. George A. Akerlof. "The Market for 'Lemons': Quality Uncertainty and the Market Mechanism." The Quarterly Journal of Economics, vol. 84, no. 3 (August, 1970). p. 495.

# ABOUT THE AUTHOR

Wade is a former golf professional, teaching professional and college golf coach that turned sales professional and sales coach and author after spending the first eighteen years of his life in golf. He has served as a branch manager for one of the top five largest privately held mortgage companies, a VP of Business Development for a local mortgage broker in Nashville TN, and has founded, developed, and sold several small businesses as an entrepreneur in Nashville.

He currently serves as a National Sales coach for a top ten Mortgage Company based in Charlotte N.C.

He and his wife of twenty years, Stephanie, and their two children, Aubrey and Aiden, live just outside of Nashville.

www.ingramcontent.com/pod-product-compliance
Lightning Source LLC
Chambersburg PA
CBHW031544210526
45464CB00003B/1147